# Puppy Training

## The Bone-ified Ultimate Step-by-Step Guide to Positive Puppy Training

### Carrie Nichole

**Digital Print House**

New York London Toronto Sydney New Delhi

assurance.

The trademarks that are used are without any consent, and the publication of the trademark is without permission or backing by the trademark owner. All trademarks and brands within this book are for clarifying purposes only and are the owned by the owners themselves, not affiliated with this document.

# Table of Contents

# Introduction

Bringing home a new puppy is hugely rewarding, and at the same time, it's a huge responsibility as well. Did you know that you, as the pet parent, are solely responsible for training him to be a responsible member of society? Did you know that failure to do so is not only a disgrace to you and a misfortune to your pup, but it could possibly land you on the wrong end of the law? Yes, it's THAT important.

But relax. Before you get in a tail-spin, owning a puppy is a privilege like none other. Your pint-size bundle of joy will be your best friend, your psychiatrist, your number one fan, your touchstone… your everything, and you will be likewise to him. There is an unbreakable bond that the two of you will develop as you go through the steps of training him. Now, thanks to this book, you can do so with confidence and ease. You can even stop to smell the roses along the way.

Thanks again for downloading this book. I hope you enjoy it!

# Chapter 1

# Warming Up

*"Happiness is a warm puppy." –*
*Charles M. Shultz*

### Are you Ready to Get Your Nose Wet?

You did it! You finally adopted that little puppy you've been dreaming of. He's absolutely adorable with his baby-soft fuzz and big, brown eyes. Your heart is just about to melt when... wait a minute... what is that he has ahold of? Could it be your favorite (and most expensive) pair of shoes? Not to worry, he only ate one. Oh... and it doesn't seem to be agreeing with him. Quick, grab some paper towels (the whole roll) and carpet cleaner. Obviously, it's time for some puppy training.

Is this your story? Did you bring the most lovable fur-ball home only to be met with one surprise after another (some being the squishy, stinky kind)? Life can certainly get hairy with a new pup, but there's no need to put your life on paws. Relax, we've got step-by-step training techniques, tried and true tips, and helpful hints to unleash the "good boy" (or girl) I know your pup can be.

You may be a bit frazzled. You may even be questioning your sanity. "What on earth was I thinking?" At best, you may be flooded with feelings of inadequacy. Then panic strikes. "I've never trained a puppy before."

It's all alright though. Your puppy has never *been* a puppy before, so the two of you can wing it together. Besides, you both have someone with bone-ified knowledge and experience in your court... me! I've trained hundreds of puppies and trained the trainers who train them too. I've helped them and I'll help you too. So, let's get rolling. You're both in for a real treat.

# First things First

There are a few subjects we must cover to set the foundation for your puppy's training. If you try to skip over any one of these, it will be like building a house on sand. It is imperative that your foundation be strong.

## Off to the Vet: A Well Tail

First, a trip to a veterinarian is in order. If you don't have one, you will need to get one. Ask friends and family members if they have a local vet they would recommend. Be sure to choose one who you like and trust. You never know when a serious matter may come along and this person may be called upon to save your dog's life. In addition, if you lean to the more natural alternative methods, try to find a vet who does the same. If you prefer mainstream traditional practices, pick a vet who does exactly that. It helps if your puppy likes his doctor, but don't count on it. Don't make that the deciding factor.

The most important thing is to secure a veterinarian and get your puppy on record. He will need some vaccinations, some of which are required, while others are simply suggested. If you are going to opt out of any, please do your homework thoroughly enough to make an informed decision on the matter. While immunizations such as Parvo are not mandatory in most locations, it's a horrible condition that can kill your pup. On the flip side, some veterinarians like to over-medicate, so have some information under your belt so you can make wise choices.

Another matter you will need to decide is whether to get your dogs spayed or neutered. Unless you have plans for your pup to reproduce, you will want to have the procedure done. No plan ensures that your dog will father or mother one or more litters, so if that is not in your plan, you must make another plan. Your vet can talk over the details and age recommendations with you, but the responsibility is yours alone.

One side note is that any surgical procedure such as spay and neutering, any illness, or any time your dog is feeling out of the usual, his training should be tailored to the situation. In most cases, potty patrol would still continue, but you are not going to want to ask him to do tricks while feeling under the weather. Needless to say, a little common sense goes a long way.

Once your pup is properly vaccinated and has a clean bill of health, it's time to get to the next subject on the list... establishing a relationship.

## Puppy Love: Relationship Matters

**Relationship.** Spending time together is everything when it comes to any relationship. The relationship between you and your new puppy is no exception. The warm, fuzzy feeling you get when you pet him and the moments you share looking into one another's eyes sets the scene, but it doesn't determine it.

Love is a state of mind, not a feeling. There will be times you may feel you have "fallen out of love" with your pup like the first time he nips you or when he stubbornly disobeys you. Love is not a feeling. Love is a state of being. Love is a commitment. Ask your puppy what love is. He knows. Dogs set the standard for love. You leave him alone all day while you go to work or go play and he's heartbroken, maybe outraged. But the moment he sees you, all is forgiven. He welcomes you back with loving paws and a big slobbery lick on the nose. No greater love exists than the love a dog has for his human.

Here are some of the most important things that will develop within your relationship:

- Spending Time Together
- Building Trust
- Establishing Pack Order

**Time.** Spending time together is a requirement for every good relationship, and the more, the better. When you first bring your puppy into your home, you will want to spend quality time together. If you can, take some days off work or school so that the two of you can bond. If that is not possible, bringing him home on your day or days off is better than during the busiest time of your week.

Keep in mind that, as mentioned earlier, your puppy has never been a puppy before. He has no idea how to act, what to do, or what to expect. It is up to you to let him know. Assure him and reassure him. When he cries at night, he is most likely missing his mother and siblings.

Giving him love and security doesn't mean you have to bend the rules. If you have established the fact that Sweetie Pie won't be sharing your bed, gently tuck him back in when he frets, just as you would a child. If the situation gets out of hand, you may have to practice a little "tough love." Let him yelp, but do so with intervals of loving pats and kind words.

Talking to your pup, taking him for walks, and just spending time together is priceless for setting a firm foundation, just like with human parenting. Yes, you read it right, the more you verbally talk to your puppy, the more he will catch on to things and the closer the two of you will become. Just as you do with a baby, say the names of things like, "ball", "water" and "walk." You may be surprised how quickly he learns the names of people, places, and things. Sing to him too; dogs love a good song, though they may howl if you sing off-key.

**Trust.** Generally, trust isn't given; it's earned. That is not usually the case with puppies though. Unless you give him a reason not to trust you, it usually comes instilled in him. He will trust you to care for him, love him, feed and water him, and teach him. Don't let him down, for being trusted is a privilege beyond measure.

**Leader of the Pack.** You've probably heard of pack order. Professional dog trainer, Ceaser Millan, made the primitive concept common knowledge. Dogs, like wolves and many other animals, are social animals set up with a "pecking order." They have a "pack mentality" that incorporates submission and dominance. He taught that by establishing yourself, the owner and trainer, as the pack leader, your dog will naturally submit; it is in his genes to do so. Whether you are a "pack" advocate or not, there is truth to the notion, as even our children are taught to follow order by way of authority. Call it what you will, but you will need to establish your leadership with love or your puppy may very well think he is the head of the household.

## Mischief vs. Malice

There's a fine line between cute puppy antics and downright bad behavior. It's imperative to nip naughtiness in the bud before it becomes a bad habit, which is harder to break than bad behavior. Below are some normal versus not-so-normal things your pup may do. Keep in mind that just because something may fall under the mischief category, it doesn't mean that you don't want to change the behavior; it simply means that it is normal for a puppy.

## Mischief

- **Chewing on Everything.** Chewing is natural for a puppy. He is teething and it's just his inborn nature to do so. You will want to prevent his access to some of his favorite chew things like your cell phone, shoes, pillows, and the kitten. Replace them with a nice doggie chew toy.

- **Jumping up on You and Everyone Else.** While jumping up is a behavior that comes with puppyhood, you will want to train him not to do so. When he does, it is a great opportunity to teach him a command such as "down" or "sit."

- **Peeing or Pooping on Your Carpet or Best Rug.** It seems like when a puppy "goes" indoors, it always takes place on your new carpet or best (and most expensive) rug. One reason may be that the texture somewhat resembles grass. Another reason may be that once he has initiated it, the scent stimulates a response in his brain telling him that is where he should "go." Not to worry. This is perfectly normal, and it is perfectly normal for you to forbid it. The fact that it is taking place in the worse possible area of the house will only speed up the process of potty training, so think of it as a positive… if you can.

## Malice

- **Guarding Food.** The act of guarding food may be an

indication that your puppy is food aggressive. While that is not an uncommon trait, it is one that can quickly get out of hand. It can be dangerous for both humans and other dogs or cats in the household, so this situation must be dealt with immediately.

- **Guarding Toys, Beds, or Possessions.** Just as in guarding food, your puppy guarding his belongings can be dangerous if he lashes out. Tend to the issue as soon as possible to prevent further complications.

- **Overly Aggressive or Timid.** Dogs definitely have personalities all their own. One will be more of an alpha male while another will be more submissive or shy. But if your puppy seems too extreme one way or the other, he probably is. However, you can modify his behavior, and if it cannot be, it is time to seek the help of a professional trainer.

- **Obsessive/Compulsive.** Some OCD behaviors are so bizarre they seem adorable. If your dog is a hoarder, for instance, it is tempting to post cute photos of the situation online and laugh it off. But the behavior may be a symptom of a major underlying problem. Do a little dog psychology and try to determine the root cause. If you have no luck, it would be good to enlist some professional help before the problem escalates.

## Safety

Safety can't be stressed enough. Your puppy's training is entirely in your hands. Even if you take him to a class or to a dog trainer, you are still the one in charge because you are choosing the individual or group of individuals who will watch over him.

If you let your pup play outside without supervision, be sure that he is fenced in, and by all means, make sure the fence is secure. Even if you are out with him, be certain that he is not able to dart out into traffic. Take it from me, I am one of the most careful, borderline-paranoid dog owners on the planet. But once, my six month-old German Shepherd, Molly, and I were playing ball in the front yard of our quiet residential neighborhood when a car came speeding down the street just as she decided to play "keep away" with the ball. The story didn't end well. Molly died in my arms. Please take your pup's safety to heart.

## Let's Get The Ball Bouncing!

Now that you have a good idea of what it takes to lay a great, solid foundation, you are now ready to take the next step. Since you are the one who will be training your puppy, you will need to be trained. Even if you are opting to have your dog professionally trained, you must do your share to keep the ball rolling, so let's move on and fetch up some "bone-ified" great training for you, the trainer.

*"A dog is the only thing on earth that loves you more than he loves himself."*

*- Josh Billings*

# Chapter 2:

# Training the Trainer

## *"I'm not spoiled. I just happen to be great at spoiling people."*

## *- Author Unknown*

Just as a teacher must be schooled before teaching school, a trainer must be trained before training his or her pup. You can establish negative behaviors by training a dog without proper training yourself, so let's take a look at the credentials you will need to be the best teacher ever. Here's what you'll need in order to train your puppy.

- Patience

- Assertiveness

- Patience

- Stick-to-it-iveness

- Patience

## Who's the Boss?

As mentioned earlier, it will be important for you to establish the fact that you are the pack leader, or "the boss" if you'd rather call it that. There is no other way. Even if part of your intention of getting a puppy was to raise him to be a guard dog, he will need to follow your commands.

If you are a quiet person with a gentle and kind demeanor, you may have to make a little adjustment in your personality. No, I don't mean you need to become mean, far from it. But you will need to take the lead, which means you must become assertive.

Even older dogs tend to be confused in certain situations. Dogs that are used to looking after a single female or an elderly person are sometimes more on edge than those who live with a clear-cut "master." You can see it in their walk and hear it in their bark. They hear a faint noise down the street or a wall cracking and they come unglued. They pull their owner when taken for a walk on a leash. Their behavior can do more harm than good often times. No, this type of assertive dog does not always belong to someone handicapped, older, or vulnerable, but in the dog's mind, the human is the weaker one when he displays such behavior. You will have to rise above your pup's vision of who you are to establish the hierarchy.

For this reason, with grace and confidence, it will be important for you to handle things in a certain way. If you have not brought your pup home yet, you are in luck. You can start the minute you bring him into your home. Enter first and then invite him in. If you already have your puppy, no problem. Each time you leave your home and come back, go in first and invite him to come in.

Likewise, when you leave the home, you exit first. This is much easier to do if he is on a leash. He'll get the message. When you feed him, have him wait before pouncing on the food. You tell him when to eat. Of course, puppies think they are starving at all times so one second is an eternity to him. Keep it fair and quick, but be the one to determine his dinner arrangements. A quick "sit" is usually sufficient for a little guy.

If you incorporate order from puppyhood, your dog will grow up to be a productive and obedient member of the household. He will display respect for you and others and will listen when you give commands. A good dog is a happy dog!

## Teaching the Teacher

If you are a student that is willing to learn, your teachable spirit will be an inspiration to both you and your puppy. Just as a parent who is open to change and suggestions can learn new and better ways, so can a dog trainer. In this section, we will focus on certain methods that have worked for the majority of dog owners and handlers, although there are exceptions to the rule.

For example, if you have a dog with a phobia of noise, you will want to take these lessons to a quiet spot. If your dog has a preoccupation with cats and your neighborhood is flocked with them, your daily walks may need to be at a spot that is cat-free like a park or another neighborhood, at least until he gets the hang of things. The same is true if you have definite preferences or limitations. You may be handicapped and unable to take daily walks, but a spin around the block in a wheelchair may be a possibility. Adaptation is a must, and the two of you will work things out a lot better if you are willing to bend and be flexible.

## Rules of the Game

Teachers have rules too, and they are often more rigid than those of their students. Why? You are the responsible party. You must lead by example. For that reason, here are a few that cannot be broken.

- **Never raise your voice.** Break the will without breaking the spirit!

- **Encourage your pup to obey.** Praise goes a long way with a pup.

- **Keep it fun.** Playing is learning to a puppy. Keeping things light and upbeat will reap rewards.

- **Time out is sometimes necessary.** If one or both of you become frustrated, hungry, or tired, it is time for a time out.

- **Respect is a must.** Mutual respect will make or break puppy training.

- **Patience is a virtue and a requirement.** There's no option. You MUST practice patience. If you don't have any, you will by the time training is underway. That is, if you play by the rules.

## Seeing Life From a Pup's Point of View

Have you ever wondered what goes on in a puppy's mind? If not, it might behoove you to do so. Just as parents get inside their child's head and a teacher attempts to wrap her head around her student's thoughts, it is good to try to imagine just what your puppy may be thinking, whether true or false.

When you are establishing your dog's boundaries and teaching him, there will be communication of some form or another. Ideally, you will ask him to "roll over," and he will oblige. Then you will embrace him and he will give you a big, fat lick on the cheek. But the situation may be quite different.

When you ask him to do something, such as come for a walk, he may stubbornly refuse. It's doubtful that it is because he doesn't want to go outdoors. He may be afraid, unsure, or downright defiant of the leash. Or, he may have an "attitude." He may be confused and think that YOU are the one who is supposed to be on the leash... that YOU have it all wrong.

A dog who refuses to heel most likely thinks that you belong on the opposite end of the lesson. One who declines to sit may be feeling like you should be the student in check. On the other side of the spectrum, your dog may be fearful or even confused.

Knowing what is going on inside his head will help you troubleshoot problems and will make puppy training a better experience. As you do so, the communication skills between the two of you will improve with leaps and bounds. He will become secure in the fact that you "get," or at least "try to get," what he is conveying. That will lead to a more submissive cooperation, a win-win situation for the both of you.

## Establishing Boundaries

There will be places that are "off limits" for your dog. There will be things that cannot be tolerated, both in actions and behaviors. Establishing these boundaries is the first step to training. It requires you, as the trainer, to determine what the rules are and then stick to them. Some things you may want to consider are:

- Where will your puppy sleep?

- Where will he play?

- How rough will he be allowed to play?

- What are his dinner-time rules?

- What must he do in order to receive a treat?

- At what point will you reprimand his barking?

- How will he be allowed to respond when there is a knock at the door?

- How will he be expected to greet visitors?

- Is he allowed on the furniture?

Making a list of rules is helpful. Start slow and establish the most important ones first. Of course, potty training is a must. We will cover that in the Chapter 4 so you might as well mark it at the top of your list.


## Conditioning

Introducing your new puppy to the world around him is essential. The way in which you do so is important too. You hold the key to help him unlock the wonders of the world in a delightful, positive way. You also have the ability, as his owner, to make a negative impact on his outlook of life. If you are fearful, he may be afraid of things too. The more balanced you are in the way you see the world and how you introduce it to your pup, the better balanced he will be as well. Here are a few helpful hints:

- Introduce him to new situations gradually but on an ongoing basis. When the trash truck is picking up the garbage, let him peek out the window and build up to walking him down the sidewalk (leashed, of course) when they are dumping cans.

- Introduce him to new people. Chances are your new pup will be a social guy and will take to everyone he meets, especially if you make it fun and exciting for him. Always expect the unexpected, especially when children are involved. Children tend to be jerky and spontaneous, which can startle a pup, and sometimes their play gets out of hand. But with careful supervision and behavior conditioning, your pup will be a social butterfly in no time.

- Your new puppy will be a bundle of energy under a layer of fur. When you anticipate he will need to be settled down for a time, like if company is coming over, do what you can to encourage him to unleash some energy - take him for a long walk, play with him for a while, or let him entertain himself with some fun toys. You will be glad you did!

## In Hind Sight – Summing it Up

With a little patience, no, make that a lot of patience, and a lot of love, you will be a terrific trainer. Who better than you, the owner, to teach your puppy? Set the rules and stick to them. Teach them one at a time, except for those that cannot be tolerated or can be tackled all at once, such as no pottying in the house, no biting, and so forth.

Don't worry if you feel unqualified. That is what you have this book for. Besides, it will keep you humble. No one likes a "know it all" and your pup is no exception. It's a journey that the two of you will embark upon. Once the ground rules are set, you will become more comfortable with implementing the rules and getting to the fun stuff.

*"It is better to know some of the questions than all of the answers"*

- *James Thurber*

# Chapter 3:

# The Classroom: Setting it Up for Success

*"If only we all were... the teacher's pet."*

*— Author Unknown (some disgruntled student somewhere)*

## Setting the Scene

Puppies are rambunctious by nature. You may have noticed that by now. They are barely still for one minute before they are onto the next thing. They are curious and playful, and there's a reason nature set it up that way; it's how they learn.

There are things that you can't change... like the energy of your pup. But you can harness it. Taking him for a nice, brisk walk before class is helpful. That will tighten your bond, establish your leadership role, and also get a little energy out of him. Hopefully he'll stay awake for his lesson, but if not, just call it "nap time" and resume once he wakes.

It's important to conduct "class" in an area where your puppy is safe and feels secure. It is also a good idea to make it free of as many distractions as possible. You don't want traffic, that's a given, nor do you need dogs barking or cats prowling about.

Once you have chosen a great location, it's best to keep class in the same setting. Your puppy will thrive on repetition and familiarity. Give him what he needs to be as comfortable as possible.

## Setting the Tone

Now that you have the location intact, set the mood. As the teacher, you will be the one that sets the tone. If you come to class with a bad attitude, guess who else is likely to have one? If you come in stressed out, your pup will pick up on that as well.

Do whatever it takes to be calm, cool, and confident. These things will set your pup's mind at ease and will do miracles for his behavior. If you are setting him up to succeed, he will!

You may want to do something that you find relaxing yet motivating just before you begin class. For some that may be enjoying a steaming cup of coffee while reading the newspaper, while others may find a walk with their pup gets them in the mode.

The same rings true for your pup. Getting him in a learning mood is important. Don't scold him right before class. If he warrants discipline, then put class off for a short while. You'll have a better student, and chances are that you will be a better teacher too.

## Timing

Just as you check your mood and that of your pup's before embarking on a lesson, there are other aspects in regards to timing that should be considered. Here are a few to think about:

- Training too close to meal time (yours or his) is not recommended.

- Training when either of you are overly tired is usually a bad idea.

- If there is a distraction, it's alright to delay class for a while.

- Keeping consistent in both the time and location of class is important.

- Try to make sure you he doesn't get involved in serious play right before class or he will be apt to have trouble adjusting.

- Don't forget to let him potty before class. Take a break during class if need be.

## Attention Span

Your puppy's attention span will be short, which is an understatement. In fact, don't be surprised if it's about the length of a millisecond at first. It should, however, grow each time you work with him. Increase his lesson by one minute each session until you have reached the desired length. Be sure to engage him. When you captivate his interest, his attention will last longer.

This is where dog breeds and temperaments come into the picture. There are some breeds that tend to be more active with lower attention spans during puppyhood and even into adulthood. Energy levels vary from pup to pup, and when your dog is preoccupied by wanting to chase his tail, it's difficult for him to concentrate.

Below is the development you can expect from your pup at given age intervals.

**Birth to 2 weeks.** During this stage of his life, known as the neonatal period, your puppy is learning to do many things like nurse, find his mother, interact with siblings, and simple coordination skills. He is also figuring out the pack process, which is known as the pecking order.

**2-4 weeks.** This span of time is the transitional period for pups. They now have their eyes open and can stand and even walk. They are developing a better sense of hearing and scent and may even bark a bit. Their teeths are beginning to come in and their tail is beginning to wag.

**4-12 weeks.** Known as the socialization period, this is the time when your puppy is capable of developing relationships with humans, other dogs, and possibly other animals as well. It is usually during this stage that a pup is ready to leave his mother and the siblings in his liter. From the fifth to seventh week, the importance of good experiences are critical, as they will play a huge factor in how the dog interacts from that time forward. During this time, your puppy will be able to focus his attention for a short time, so take advantage of the times he is willing to learn.

It is around the seventh week that your puppy may be able to begin potty training. This may be a bit complicated by the fact that from weeks eight to ten he is likely to be fearful. It is a normal process that should be over and done with around the end of the tenth week, which is why many find the ninth to twelfth weeks the prime time to potty train. By this time, your puppy is most likely willing to pay attention and cooperate within reason.

**3-6 months.** Ahhh... the ranking period. This is a crucial time within your pup's development for a number of reasons. He is discovering more and more about the pack, both human and dogs, he is around. This phase is often equated with elementary school age because he is developing both socially and educationally. This is a wonderful time to be training your dog, as he will be better able to listen and learn than ever before and for longer lengths of time. Beware that around the fourth month, he may go through a short "fear" spree in which he is once again afraid of things or people. During this time, a little reassurance will go a long way.

**6-18 months.** Now things are really coming together for your puppy. He is "getting" the hierarchy protocol of the pack, which may entail yourself, you and other humans, or possibly both humans and dogs. Much of the way he acts and reacts will be determined by his interaction within the group, or pack. He most likely will buck the system a bit and challenge you or others at times, but this is just part of his growing up. Don't be afraid to assert your authority in a kind and loving manner. Dogs that aren't "fixed" will usually begin to show some sexual mannerisms, which may cause complications during training, as they may be distracted at times, like when a dog of the opposite sex is nearby. Otherwise, your puppy should be like putty in your hand, ready to be molded into a smart and obedient dog.

**18 months-2 years.** It is within this time frame that you can really see the dog your pup is becoming. Many people forget that a dog is still a puppy during this time, even though their size may mislead you. They are becoming more mature and trainable, but until two, and even three years of age, they are not quite adults.

# Class Outside of the Classroom

There will be many times when your lessons will take place outside the classroom. Potty training, behavioral training, and life lessons are bound to happen at any given moment, so be sure to establish a great teacher-student relationship, not only in the classroom, but outside of it as well. Teach your pup from an early age to listen to your voice, your tone, and to acknowledge when you are instructing him, inside and outside of class.

## The Sum of It All

When you are both knowledgeable and in tune with your puppy, you will get a good feel for what the requirements will be to train him. You will have one set and he will have yet another. Your attitude, mood, classroom setting, and of course, training knowledge will greatly determine whether lessons are a pass or fail. Your pup will require patience, understanding, firmness, and repetition, along with being aware of his attention span abilities. Training your dog is a privilege that with the help of this book, you will be able to handle with dignity and grace. So, dig in… and get ready to make leaps and bounds in the wonderful step-by-step sessions that lie ahead.

*"No home décor is complete without dog hair."*

*-Posted on Pinterest*

# Chapter 4:

# Potty Training Your Puppy

*"But the cat gets to poop in the house."*

*– said the Dog about the Cat*

"Yay… it's time to potty train my dog," said no dog owner ever. But unless your dog is to never enter a human domain, he must be trained. While he may balk at the idea because, after all, the cat is not made to go out in the freezing snow to relieve himself and the humans are allowed to do it in the "big water bowl," your dog may not quite understand why he is subjected to such punishment, but you must still plug away with the task at hand.

## How it Works

There are a number of methods to the madness. Finding the one that works for you and your puppy will be determined by your own individual dog and your situation. Some dogs are more easily trained than others due to temperament and breed. Others have easy access to the outdoors and have a human with them for most of the day, which, of course, makes training more simplified. But no matter your dog's breed or personality or your situation, the methods are tried and true and one will surely work for you.

# Puppy Potty Training Tips

Potty training can be a mess, literally, but it can also be rewarding. This is most likely the first leg of your training journey. You will, no doubt, experience frustration and despair. Your dog will probably do the same. But when the paperwork is over and it's time to examine the end result, the two of you will have bonded and feel proud of the outcome. Here are a few tried and true tips that can help you along when housetraining your pup.

- Remember to reward your puppy for "going" in the designated area.

- Consistency, positive reinforcement, and patience will get you the desired results.

- Puppies' bladders are small, so take him out often, once upon waking and every 30 minutes thereafter, if possible, and then again before bedtime.

- A routine feeding schedule is ideal, as he will be more apt to "go" at regular intervals.

- Take him to the exact same place every time.

- Take note of his elimination schedule and try to accommodate it.

- Never scold your pup for having an accident.

- Limiting his water before bed is a fantastic idea.

- Put his food dish up in between meals to establish a routine.

- Know that there will be accidents and keep pushing towards the goal.

- He aims to please.  Praise goes a long, long, long way!

# When He's Got to Go, He's Got to Go... Things to Watch For

There are certain tell-tale signs that may indicate your puppy needs to go potty.  Here are some of the most common ones to watch for.


- Getting antsy

- Sneaking around

- Going behind a chair or other secluded location

- Heading towards the door


# Housetraining Techniques

### Signs of the Time

This method requires keeping a constant eye on your pup.

1. When you see him show signs of needing to "go," quickly lead him to the designated potty area.

2. If he does potty, lavishly praise him and give him a treat of some form if you chose to do so.

3. If he does not go immediately, give him some more time to produce.

4. If he still doesn't perform, take him back inside or

wherever you were before the false alarm occurred and keep an eye peeled for squirming or any signs that he needs to go try again. In the event that he does, go back to step 1.

## Midstream

This method is actually an add-on to the above method or any other method you choose. In other words, it is designed to complement another form of training.

1. If you see your pup having an accident, pick him up (carefully). If he is pooping, wait until he is through and follow through with these steps. It is doubtful that you will get further poop, but it will still teach him and he still may need to pee.

2. The idea is to startle him a bit so he stops peeing, but not so much that it frightens him.

3. Place him in his designated potty spot and wait until he relieves himself the rest of the way.

4. Praise him and offer him a treat if you choose to do so.

5. If he does not continue his business, wait patiently, and if he still doesn't, take him back to where you were before the incident, clean up, and watch for tell-tale signs of him needing to go again.

## Ring the Bell

This is a fun and often effective method of potty training. It seems to be easier for pups that are a little older, but even if you have a young one, you might want to give it a whirl.

1. For this method, you will need a bell, such as a doorbell. You can get a regular one or a fancy one made for dogs. The choice is yours.

2. Let your dog become familiar with the bell.

3. Teach him to ring it and deliver a treat when he does so.

4. Next, mount it on the wall near the door and have him ring it. Again, reward him for doing so.

5. Then you will want to transition to teaching him to ring the bell so the door will be opened.

6. The first time or two that he rings it in the new location, reward him and let him out.

7. Then, simply let him out when he rings the bell. It may be a little while before he associates going outside with pottying because at first it may be simply for fun and games, but he'll get the idea eventually.

*"So early in my life, I had learned that if you want something, you had better make some noise." – Malcolm X*

## Away For a Time

There will be times when you can't be at home or are at home but cannot constantly monitor your pup for signs that he needs to go potty. You may work from home, have young children to attend to, or have company. Who knows, you may just need a break. Here is one way you can handle the situation:

1. Acquire a nice size pen or gate in an area for your pup.

2. Be sure to make it pleasant with water, his toys, his

bed, and maybe a treat or two.

3. Lay a newspaper on the floor, and when he makes a puddle or poopie elsewhere, sit him on the paper. You can also opt for using a doggie litter box that has Astroturf grass on top but allows the pee to drain into a catch hole.

4. When he does pee or poop on the paper, praise him and reward him with a treat if desired.

5. It will take a lot of repeats, but he will finally get the hint.

## Non-Compliance Warning Signs

If your puppy is not cooperating, there may be underlying reasons. He may just be stubborn. Some breeds are simply bull-headed, such as Basset Hounds. Other breeds are slow learners.

It could also be your pup's temperament or development. If he is high strung or is the runt and is running behind in maturity, cut him some slack. He'll catch on.

There may also be medical reasons that he is having problems. He could have a bladder infection or a number of other conditions. Dogs that are fixed, especially females, can develop complications that cause them to have difficulty holding their bladder. On the opposite side of the spectrum, dogs that aren't fixed, mainly males, often have the overwhelming desire to "mark" their areas. A trip to the vet is in order if any of these problems are suspected.

## It Will All Come Out Just Fine

At times, puppy potty training will get hairy. You may want to just give up and let the pee (and poop) fall where it may. Your puppy will most likely feel the same way. But don't give up, and never give in.

By trying out the tried and true techniques mentioned in this chapter, you and your dog are sure to find one that fits. Watch for signs that he needs to go then implement the method of your choice. When he produces, praise him fully and reward with a treat if you are going that route.

Potty training is most likely the first training the two of you will embark on, and it's likely to be the most important one as well. On the bright side, once your pup "gets it," he will truly "get it."

*"You can't pee like a puppy if you wanna run with the big dogs." – Nikki Sixx*

# Chapter 5:

# Obedience Expedience: The "Pawsitive Puppy" Behavioral Crash Course

*"Obedience is an act of faith; disobedience is the result of unbelief." - Edwin Louis Cole*

Obedience is a must. People must follow rules and so must dogs, even puppies. Some negative behaviors are forbidden. There will be some rules that they will need to learn right away, for their sake, for yours, and for everyone's sake around them. Teaching them obedience is your responsibility and your privilege as well.

Consistency and repetition will boost your pup's confidence. He will find security in knowing what to expect. Don't let him down. You, and only you, can make a believer out of your young pup… in a good way, of course.

Below you will find suggested and required obedience subject matter and step-by-step instructions for some of the most important things to teach your puppy in order for him to be an acceptable member of society. By the way, welcome to the wonderful world of puppy obedience training!

## Know the Rules

It is usually the town or city that you live in that governs the regulations about dogs. If you live in a community within the town or city, certain restrictions may also apply. Although rural residences are usually much more lax in their regulations, you will still find at least the basic ones still apply. Here are some of the legalities you may find in your area.

- **Breed Restrictions.** Some geographical locations do not allow certain breeds. Denver, Colorado and Miami, Florida do not allow Pit Bulls in the city. Other areas allow the breed but require a specific amount of insurance coverage on them. Many apartments have breed and size restrictions. Unfortunately, we don't have a solution to any of these regulations except for the one about carrying insurance, in which case the lessons in this chapter can help you prevent the need to use it.

- **Tags and Immunizations.** A good number of areas have ordinances requiring that your dog be tagged and licensed and that he have certain immunizations, including rabies.

- **Aggression.** You are legally responsible for preventing your pet from posing as a threat to the community. This includes aggressive behavior towards humans and other animals. Even the best behaved pup likes a good kitty chase, so the important lessons in this chapter will help prevent a possible tail-spin of trouble.

- **Nuisance.** In most areas, you must take responsibility to assure your pet is not a nuisance to others. This includes trash scavenging, constant barking, and so forth. Oh, and add terrorizing the mailman to this list. Yes, obedience training is a must!

# Know the Risks

Breaking the rules and regulations have consequences for both the owner and the dog, even if your dog is a puppy. Fines, doggie jail, and even having your dog taken away from you can be the result of your failure to follow the legalities where you live. Don't look back in hind sight with regret, let's get to the solution: puppy obedience training.

# Training Tips

- Keep calm and train your dog. He will quickly pick up on your calm, cool and, collective demeanor or… your tailspin. He will be apt to mirror your state of mind, so it's best to take whatever measures are needed to remain calm and positive at all times.

- The words that are used in all of the lessons within this book are the ones that I have chosen. Feel free to use your own. I once worked with a police service dog whose commands had to be given in German. You can use whatever words or language you want, as long as you keep them consistent so you and your pup are on the same page.

- Getting on your hands and knees so you are on your pup's level is often helpful. Imagine yourself looking up at a giant to follow his instructions and you will see why it might be the best angle for puppy training.

- Repeat and repeat! Repetition is a must. Doing the same thing over and over will help your puppy become a pro. If your puppy seems to tire of repeating the lesson, add a wrinkle like a change in treats or location or even a slight twist to the trick.

- Never forget to reward your puppy. Puppies thrive on attention, praise, and of course, on treats. Whatever you chose for your system is fine, as long as you remember to reward him each and every time he successfully does as he is asked. As he grows up a bit, your pup can be expected to carry out many of your requests/commands without being rewarded. Initially, however, you will want to reward him for most every good behavior. It's much like child training. A child is taught to do thing like putting his or her dirty clothes in the laundry and is praised or rewarded for doing so at first but as he or she gets older, it is just expected. The same holds true in many things with your pup.

## Training Treats

All pups love to get treats, but some simply don't need them. If your puppy is on the pudgy side or you worry about him getting treat overload, there are some great options.

For one, there are micro-treats that suffice the purpose but aren't a full-size goodie so the calorie count is lower. You can also opt to give him a single kibble of his regular puppy food. Praise should always accompany a treat and actually can be lavished in lieu of one, as can a favorite toy.

## Puppy Obedience Training 101

### Sit

While this is one of the most basic dog obedience lessons in existence, it may be the most important. Not only is it adorable to see your pup sit on command, but it's also good manners, and in an emergency, may just save his life. If a car is coming and he's veering towards the street, you can tell him to sit. Even pups who have learned to "heel" or "stay" seem to respond to "sit" more quickly than other commands.

Once he gets the hang of this one, try it in an emergency drill to see how he does with it under those conditions.

1. Get on level with your pup and hold a treat near his nose.

2. Verbally tell him to "sit."

3. Move the treat slowly so that he follows it with his eyes.

4. Gradually move your hand up, which will encourage his bottom to lower into a sitting position. Be sure not to hold it too high or he will want to jump up for it.

5. He may need a little help as his bottom lowers to make it into a full sitting position, but let him get close on his own.

6. Once his bottom makes contact with the ground, allow him to have the treat.

7. Praise your pup for being the smartest, most obedient puppy that ever graced the planet. You should both see eye-to-eye on that one!

**Sit and Stay**

Pups seem to learn to "stay" easier when they "sit" first. The action of sitting stops them in their tracks and gives them a specific position to "stay" in. It is particularly useful when a distraction is on the horizon, such as a cat. Having your puppy to sit before being told to stay diverts some attention and energy so his puppy-mania doesn't get the best of him. The same is true for even more dangerous situations like an oncoming car when simply sitting won't do the trick. It is equally important for him to stay in the position.

The first of the lesson is just a quick overview of the above "sit" lesson.

1. Loosely place a leash around your pup's neck. Give him a minute or two to get used to it.

2. Have your pup sit by enticing him with a tantalizing treat above his nose that lures him back into a sitting position.

3. When his rear-end is successfully on the ground, reward him with the treat.

4. Praise him then tell him to "stay."

5. Signal for him to "stay" by waving your flat palm toward him.

6. Repeat, "Stay."

7. Make a movement such as stepping in front of your dog. If he does not move, reward him. If he does, put him back in place.

8. Give his command again. "Stay!"

9. Make another movement. If he remains in place, reward him. If not, move him back into place.

10. Once he has successfully completed the lesson a time or two, release him by saying "Okay."

11. Reward your puppy for his excellence, but if excellence was not reached, mentally make a note to go over the lesson again soon while parts of it are still in his memory.

**Stay**

It's a good idea to teach your dog to "stay" from positions other than just his sitting position. The situation may arise that it is not appropriate for him to sit before staying, such as a time he may be treading over a cactus patch or a water puddle.

1. Gently put a loose leash around his neck and allow him to get used to it for a short time.

2. Whatever position he is in, tell him to "stay." Also give him the flat palm signal that is also his cue to "stay."

3. Make a movement such as walking in front of him or beside him.

4. If he stays in place, reward him with praise and a treat. If not, put him back in position.

5. Repeat several times.

**Come**

The mailman just pulled up and you and your pup are getting out of the car and heading to the front door when he suddenly stops. You should have leashed him, even for such a short and simple trek, but you didn't. The situation could easily get out of hand, as your puppy's teeth are now sharp as a razor blade, and he loves to use them... especially on something as tasty as... the mailman!

Don't let this scenario happen to you. Be prepared. Here's the way you do it:

1. Place a leash lightly around your puppy's neck.

2. Kneel down in front of him and say, "Come."

3. If he comes to you, reward and praise him.

4. If he doesn't come to you, reach out and give a gentle tug to his leash so that he comes to you. Reward and praise him.

5. When he's got the hang of the lesson, take it to the next level by standing further from him and repeating it.

6. Now it's time to make it a little trickier. Wait until he is preoccupied and then tell him to "come." If he does, it's time for some super great rewarding, but if not... give it another try.

## Down

Puppies love to jump on people. To your pup, it's just the natural thing to do. But to you and to your children or visitors, it's obnoxious and potentially dangerous. Imagine your great-grandma coming over only to be knocked down by your adorable, bouncing baby puppy. Don't let your puppy be the cause of grandma's broken back or a child's scrapped knee. Teach him before disaster strikes.

### Method 1: Catching Him in the Act

1. When your puppy jumps on you or someone else, give him the command, "Down." Also give him the hand command, which is your open palm pointed towards the ground.

2. If he obeys, give him plenty of praise and a treat as well. And yes, while your pup is a pup, you might want to keep treats in your pockets at all times.

### Method 2: Creating the Act

1. Secure a treat in your hand and let your pup sniff it.

2. Now, move your hand towards the ground so that he follows the treat.

3. When he has followed it to the ground, say, "Down." If he remains down, give him the treat along with praise.

4. Repeat the exercise, this time hiding the treat in your hand. If he does it successfully, give him the treat and praise, otherwise, try again.

## Leash Etiquette and Safety

A walk with your dog can be the most pleasurable experience, but it could also be the worst. Your dog may be on a leash you're holding, but that doesn't mean that things can't go wrong, very wrong.

Not only might your pup decide he has gone far enough and refuse to go another inch, but he might also might trip you up or even escape the leash. And… there's always that pup that wants to take his human for a walk. If you have ever had a nice walk go bad, you know exactly what I am talking about. But there are lessons you can implement in order to make sure your next walk around the block is a success and not a walk of shame, for you or your dog.

### Getting Off on the Right Foot (and Paw)

Hopefully you and your puppy will take many wonderful walks together. Help establish on-leash walking to be an excellent experience for you both by following the steps below.

1. Place the leash on your pup and allow him to get used

to it.

2. Gently lead him with the leash.

3. Take small, slow steps at first.

4. Encourage him to walk along with you at first, but don't worry about having him sit or heel. There's plenty of time for that after he learns to go with the flow, at least part of the time.

5. Praise him for walking and give him occasionally treats. Soon enough, you will want to halt the treats so walking can become his treat.

## Heel

Heeling is when your dog walks alongside you. In keeping with the "pack order," he should ideally be just behind, and definitely not in front of you. Here's how it's done:

1. Leash your pup and let him have a minute to get used to it.

2. Place him on your left side and have him sit.

3. As you begin to walk, use the leash to encourage him to walk at your side. At this time, say, "heel."

4. If he decides to pull, let him reach the end of the leash and tell him to "heel" while correcting him gently with the leash.

5. Likewise, if he lags behind, do the same.

6. If your pup is preoccupied with not following beside you, take a u-turn and throw him off guard. Use the leash to guide him while telling him to "heel."

7. Each and every time he does obey, shower him with

praises and give him a treat.

## Leash Logic

If your pup isn't taking too well to the leash, there are a number of things you might look into. Below is a list of things to consider.

- Is the leash or collar the right fit? There are all shapes and types of both, so be sure that the collar fits nicely, not too loose and not too tight, and that it is not too thin or thick. You can get halter-type leashes and many other problem-solving types as well.

- Is it the location that you are walking in that is causing the issue? Some dogs are scared of traffic, other dogs, or too many people. Is the noise too loud for him? Be sure the environment you are walking in is conducive to a successful walk.

- Timing is important. If he is too hungry, tired, or wound up, it's doubtful he will have a good walk, and the same is true if you are in need of destressing, dinner, or a nap.

## Commanding vs. Requesting

When addressing dog or puppy training, the question always comes up, "Should I give a command or request?" Asking your puppy to do a certain activity is, of course, the preferred method. It is a polite and mannerly way to get your dog to cooperate. Or… not. Some dogs and pups alike tend to need a little more assertiveness, just as some children do. The main thing is that you are not overbearingly demanding or strict on them, as that can damage a dog's self-esteem and even give way to his rebellion.

But you also can't ask him to do something and take "no" for an answer any more than a parent can ask a child to not play in the street and be alright with anything less than full compliance. So the choice is yours regarding how you want to coin the phrase, but the ultimate goal remains to train your puppy, and the ultimate mannerism must remain the same as well. You must train him with respect and positivity.

## Noise Control

An intruder enters your home and your puppy's barking alerts the neighbors, who are alert to the fact that something is wrong. They call the police and… your life is saved. However, this is the exception to the rule.

The scenario is usually more like this: The doorbell rings and your dog sets off into a barking frenzy. This is completely natural behavior, obnoxiously natural, that is.

Excessive barking is annoying and it can get you in trouble with the law too. Here are some ways that you can embark on some "no bark" exercises.

- Ignore your puppy's barking until he stops. Once he has stopped the behavior, give him affection and a treat. As you do so, tell him, "Quiet." It is imperative that he realizes he is being rewarded for NOT barking.

- Distract his interest by giving him a toy or treat that he can put into his mouth. This will make it difficult, if not impossible, for him to bark. Once he isn't attempting to bark, say, "Quiet." Then, lavish him with more love and treats.

- When you have taught him to "speak," you will also teach him to "quiet" so you can use that command as well.

## Tie a Yellow Ribbon… Or Not

You may have heard of the Yellow Dog Project or seen its Facebook page. The non-profit organization advocates tying a yellow ribbon around a dog's collar if he is in need of a little (or a lot) improvement in his behavior. There are definitely pros and cons in doing so.

Children love to pet puppies. But not all pups like to be petted, and the same is true for older dogs. A yellow ribbon is an indicator that people and other animals should proceed with caution. That can be a great thing if you pup likes to nip or is afraid of other dogs. But it can be a not-so-good thing too. Here's why…

In some states, having a sign that says "Beware of Dog" is a scary thing, in that it indicates that you are aware that your dog is dangerous. That places full responsibility on you. In many places, it is perfectly legal for anyone to shoot at a dog that is felt to be a danger. Yes… "felt to be." A yellow ribbon, to some, is like hanging a bull's eye on your dog.

Of course, the situation varies according to where you are and what you are doing and where your dog is… and what he is doing. If he is roaming around the countryside with a yellow ribbon on, some may interpret it to mean that he is dangerous, even though it may only signal that he is a new pup and therefore should be treated with caution. Then again, if you are going to the park or dog park, the ribbon may denote exactly what you intend.

If you are going to tie a yellow ribbon, please do so with consideration to the "what ifs", both positive and negative. Like many other areas of your pup's life, the things you do, or don't do, make a huge impact.  Sometimes you just have to dig in, find out the facts, and go with your gut.


## Dog Obedience Summary Unleashed

While training your dog to jump hoops and dance for treats is an option, teaching him to be a responsible member of society is not.  It is your duty as a dog owner to be sure that he is trained in that arena.  The consequences for being out of control are many, and include fines, unwelcome stays in the slammer (possibly for both you and your dog), and the ultimate horror of losing custody of your pup.  Doing the right thing will not only prevent such drastic measures, as those that can be taken against you both if you don't, but it's also a building block to step on for many enjoyable training lessons to come.

> *"Dogs teach us a very important lesson in life.  The mailman is not to be trusted." – Sian Ford*

# Chapter 6:

# Teaching a New Pup Old Tricks

*"Training a puppy is like raising a child. Every single interaction is a training opportunity."*

*- Ian Dunbar*

When training your dog, it's important to do so in every interaction you have with him. In teaching him not to beg, you don't want to turn right around and give him a bite of food off your dinner plate. The same is true not only of teaching him manners but fun things as well. If you are teaching him to play ball and he brings you the ball with playful, brown eyes, oblige him. You don't have to every single time, but if he wants to learn, be sure to take him up on it.

## Seize the Day

When your dog is a puppy, he is full of wonder. Although he is a ball of energy, he is a blank slate as well. Teaching him at an early age is optimal. Just like with humans, it's easier in the long run to teach a youngster than it is to teach an older dog, as they usually have to unlearn things first, such as learning not to run off with the ball. So, seize the day, grab your pup and… let's play, the learning way!

## Fun Tricks

Fun tricks are meant to be… well, fun. Unlike obedience training lessons, these lessons are not so much for safety and manners as they are for being ridiculously cute. The more your pup see that he steals the show when he performs them, the more he will want to do them and learn more. Let's get started, shall we?

## Shake

It just doesn't get any cuter than a puppy who greets someone with a shake of his paw. Make your dog a star and a mannerly member of society as well.

1. Have him assume a sitting position.

2. Get his attention while showing him a treat tucked in your hand (that shouldn't be difficult to do).

3. Now close your hand so that he cannot see the treat but is still aware of it.

4. Lift is paw a little and say, "Shake."

5. If he lifts it at all, give him the treat. If not, lift it for him but do not reward him until he shows even a slight indication that he "gets" it.

6. Continue to work with him. If he doesn't cooperate, try again later. If he does, repeat a few times so that it etches in his memory. Lavish him with love and give him a delicious treat.

7. After he has mastered this trick, get him used to shaking with others in the family, visitors, and even random people at the park. He will love the attention he'll get.

## High Five

This trick is just a fun twist of "shake." The method used to teach it is basically the same, and the outcome, just a little more hip.

1. Have your dog sit. Tuck a treat inside your closed hand and let him sniff it.

2. Lift his paw slightly and say, "High Five."

3. Hold your hand out with the inside of your hand ready to "high five" him.

4. Reward him for any indication he gives that he wants to "high five."

5. When he makes contact with your hand, let him know that he is the best, smartest, most terrific pup ever!

## Roll Over

If you want your pup to land the starring role, he must learn to roll. This one can be a bit tricky, but don't despair, once he gets it down, he'll soon be up for an Academy Award and will oblige all encores that are requested.

1. Get on your pup's level and coax him to get down to as close to a laying position as possible, while holding a treat right under his nose in your up-facing open palm.

2. Tell him to "roll over" in a fun, firm, and positive voice.

3. Display the treat in a side-winding way that encourages him to become a bit unbalanced so that he flops to his side.

4. Reward him for flopping.

5. Repeat the exercise, but add a new twist. Just as he

flops, keep the treat moving so that he rolls over. If he follows the cue and rolls over, treats and praises are in order for sure! If not, keep trying!

## Play Dead

Talk about a show! Once your puppy masters this exercise, you can add to the drama by pointing your finger at him so he plays dead on cue.

1. From a "down" position, give your pup a nice belly rub to calm him down.

2. Gently roll him to one side and give him praise and a small treat.

3. Say, "Play dead."

4. Repeat several times and then add in a little more to the scene by telling him to "stay." When he does, give him more treats. If he doesn't, put him back in position.

5. Each time you do the drill with him, get him to stay longer.

## Fetch

Most dogs will engage in a nice game of fetch. It's the bringing it back and releasing that stumps him, and rightfully so. But this lesson will have him completing the trick full circle.

1. Toss a ball, bone, or toy a small distance from your dog. He most likely will go after it, but if not, encourage him to do so by going after it yourself while

calling him.

2. Once he gets the object, call him to you. If he comes, reward him. If he takes off with the object, continue to call him until he comes while enticing him with a treat.

3. Getting him to let go of the object is tricky at first, so exchange it for a treat. The next time, have him give you the object and then reward him.

4. You will want to promote the treat of this game as being the game itself. When he releases the object to you, you toss it again and he gets to go after it. Until he "gets" that, you will need to give treats and praise as he goes along.

**Dance a Jig**

Dancing comes more natural to some pups, just as it comes more natural to some people. Poodles and small breeds seem to have a knack for this activity. If your dog balks at dancing, don't make him. Some breeds are prone to hip disorders so it might be Mother Nature looking out for him.

1. Dangle a treat above your pup's head so that he has to get on his hind legs to reach it.

2. Move the treat around and say, "Dance."

3. As he sways and moves with your motions, give him love and a treat.

**Speak and Quiet**

Your pup was born a social creature. Teaching him to "speak" isn't as difficult as you may think.

1. Get a treat or toy and capture your puppy's attention with it.

2. Keep it out of his reach but say, "Speak."

3. Work on getting him excited, which will trigger a noise, at least eventually. Then, reward him.

4. After he gets the hang of "speaking," teach him to stop by saying, "Quiet." When he does, reward him again.

## Icing on the Treat

Owning a dog is an awesome mix of pain and pleasure. Just as with parenting a child, you will spend a good bit of time teaching him right from wrong, kosher from un-kosher, acceptable from non-acceptable. Training him is one of the most rewarding things you will do with your pup, and while obedience training is a necessary part of responsible pet parenting, teaching him fun tricks is just icing on the cake, or the on treat, you might say.

*"If you're uncomfortable around my dog, I'm happy to lock you in the other room when you come over." - Author Unknown*

# Chapter 7:

# Fun and Unique Puppy Lessons

*"Whoever said you can't buy happiness forgot about puppies." - Will Rogers*

## Pick a Trick

These are super fun tricks for both you and your pup. Treat them as such and you'll have one happy puppy. It's good to infiltrate one or more into his regular obedience lessons... just for the fun of it!

### Backwards Boogie

This little jig is adorable, especially if you put on a little music. I like telling the kids it is "backwards day" and letting my pup put on the show.

1. Have your pup stand still while you wave a treat near his nose.
2. Take a step towards him, which will nudge him backwards. While doing so, say, "Back."
3. When he goes backwards even the slightest bit, give him love and a treat.
4. If you have trouble getting him to step backward, hold a box in front of him and take a small step towards him.
5. When he gets it down, repeat several times.

**The Bouncing Ball**
Nothing is as fun as watching your puppy chase a bouncing ball; he will jump up as it bounces high into the air. Teaching him to catch it and bring it back to you takes talent, so let's get the ball bouncing.
1. Familiarize your puppy with a ball.
2. Toss the ball and encourage him to go for it.
3. Tell him to "fetch" the ball.
4. When he brings it back, shower him with praise and a treat.

**Opening and Shutting the Door**
This little trick can actually save you from having to get up and down all day. Plus, it's ingenious!
1. Tie a little strip of cloth to a door knob.
2. Encourage your dog to take an interest in it.
3. Tell your dog to "open." Encourage your dog to tug at the cloth until it opens the door, then give him plenty of praise and treats.
4. Likewise, once he has mastered opening it, help him tug the cloth to shut the door when you say, "Close." Generously give him praise and treats for that as well.

**Salute**
If you have a friend or family member who is or was in the service, this is a fabulous trick to teach your pup.
1. Have your dog lie down.
2. Gently place a sticky note or piece of tape to his fur just above his eye.
3. Tell him to "salute."
4. When he goes to remove it with his paw, reward him.
5. After several rounds of success, do the lesson without the sticky item by just touching above his eye. Reward him for cooperating.
6. Now do the drill with no props or touching, and when

he follows through, let him know he is the best and smartest puppy ever.  He will agree.

## Summing up the Fun

The tricks in this chapter are for sheer pleasure.  They will probably be your pup's favorite ones.  Training your dog develops a deep bond, as does playing together, so with these tricks, you get the best of both.

# Chapter 8:

# Troubleshooting Techniques

*"Remember this: You are the expert of your body."*

*–Sarah Hackley*

Being a pet parent is indeed one of the true joys of life, and when your pet is a puppy, it's the best of time. Or... all the worse, in some cases. If you are discovering to your dismay that your puppy is not the scholar you hoped for and that his citizenship in class and perhaps even his academic level is less than you hoped for, rest assured that I have some excellent information that can help you troubleshoot your training, and the trainee as well.

## Professional Help

If your pup is showing any signs of being completely disinterested or unable to do any of the lessons, it's time to seek some help.

A trip to the vet is in order. He will need to be checked for diseases, as well as his physical and mental development. Don't panic. Even dogs with disorders make fine pets, but it is important to know about any limitations.

You may also want to enlist the help of a professional dog trainer. He will be able to spot any problems that may be standing in the way between your pup and his potential.

Just as human parents do, you love your puppy unconditionally. After all, you have learned that from him. So if your pup is slow in learning or if he is just an unruly student, time and patience will be key in training your dog, and yourself, to be the best the two of you can be.

**The Tail End**

> *"Love is…wet noses, slobbery kisses and a wagging tail."*
> *- Every Pet Parent Everywhere*

# Conclusion

Thank you again for downloading this book!

I hope this book gave you some fun and insightful information concerning training your new puppy. While life with a puppy can be as warm and fuzzy as your brand new ball of fuzz, it can also get hairy. This book is your manual to training your pup to be the wonderful creature he was put on this earth to be.

May you have endless hours of bonding with your new best friend with rewarding lessons accomplished and plenty of terrific tricks to show off. May your heart be full and your lap... never be empty.

Finally, if you enjoyed this book, then I'd like to ask you for a favor. Please be kind enough to leave a review of this book on Amazon? It'd be greatly appreciated!

Click here to leave a review for this book on Amazon!

Thank you and good luck!

## Preview of *"Brain Games for Dogs: Training, Tricks and Activities for your Dog's Physical and Mental wellness"*

# Chapter 1: Introducing Brain Games

Brain games are the latest craze. Studies show that these fun games are very effective ways to enhance learning skills and improve memory too. Brain games for humans are steadily gaining in popularity but the ones for the family pooch adds a whole new tailspin on the subject.

What are brain games for dogs? Just as they do for humans, brain games provide endless hours of entertainment and sharpen the mind at the same time. They are games that provoke thinking, problem solving, memory and other skills that exercise the brain. But, of course, the difference is, they are designed for dogs.

While crossword puzzles, Rubik's cubes, Sudoku and Memory are favorite brain games for humans, dogs prefer ones of a slightly different nature. Canines love running, jumping, treats and affection, so it just makes sense that when embarking on games that will enhance your dog's brain that you do so with the goal of captivating his interests also. After all, you can't really send your pup to time out for not participating in them, so it's imperative to get his attention to gain his willing cooperation.

How do dog brain games work? First, let's examine how a dog's brain works. In many ways, a canine's brain resembles that of a human's. For one, both are social creatures, which means that there is a portion of both human and dog brains devoted to social-related information processing. Neural control mechanisms in both brains possess verbal auditory awareness in verbal communication. That is to say they both have "voice areas". While dogs cannot actually engage in verbal communication, like conversations, as humans do, studies prove that they do comprehend much of what is said to them. Not only that, they detect the meanings of tones as well. Dog owners can attest to the fact that their dog knows their voice, their tone and usually, the underlying meaning behind what is being said.

Love is another thing humans and dogs share. While love is an emotion, it originates in the brain. Brain scans have even been performed that confirm that love stems from the same part of the brain in both canines and humans. Likewise, the part of the brain where positive emotions come from called the caudate nucleus, a part of the brain associated with positive emotions called the caudate nucleus is quite similar in both species.

While a dog's brain is actually only about one tenth the size of a human brain, the analogous

structures are much like a humans'. They have very similar brain waves, and in dreaming. If you have a dog, you have probably noted him paddling his hind legs as if he is running or even whining in his sleep. Dogs have memories, too. He may not be up to recalling his whole week or year as humans are able to do, but he certainly recognizes people, places and things. Many dogs get very excited when in route to a favorite spot. He begins to see and smell things that are familiar along the way and kicks into high gear, anticipating where he is going.

Yet one more aspect that the two brains have in common is the fact that when an area of the brain is neglected, it becomes less useful or of no use at all. Like muscles that are not working, the function is eventually lost. That is why brain games are so important in both humans and dogs. It's like "use it or lose it", as the old saying goes. As a dog owner, it is up to you to keep your four-legged friend's brain active and alive. After all, he would do the same for you and in many ways, he already does. Research shows that dogs stimulate human brains also, so it's only right to stimulate his in return.

**Click here to check out the rest of _Brain Games for Dogs: Training, Tricks and Activities for your Dog's Physical and Mental wellness"_ on Amazon.**

# Check Out My Other Books

Below you'll find some of my other popular books that are popular on Amazon and Kindle as well. Simply click on the links below to check them out. Alternatively, you can visit my author page on Amazon to see other work done by me.

**Train Your Dog like a Pro:The Ultimate Step by Step Guide on How to Train a Dog in obedience**

**Dog Obedience Training -An Easy and Effective Step-by-Step Guide to Train Your Dog Positively**

## References:

http://iheartdogs.com/do-you-know-what-a-yellow-ribbon-tied-on-a-dogs-collar-means-you-should/?utm_content=bufferfac05&utm_medium=social&utm_source=facebook.com&utm_campaign=buffer

http://pets.webmd.com/dogs/guide/house-training-your-puppy

Do You Know What A Yellow Ribbon Tied On A Dog's Collar ...

iheartdogs.com

Made in the USA
Middletown, DE
19 August 2020